Everyday Superheroes
WOMEN IN STEM CAREERS

Erin Twamley

AND

Joshua Sneideman

WISE Ink
CREATIVE ★ PUBLISHING

Paperback ISBN: 978-1-63489-198-1
Hardcover ISBN: 978-1-63489-204-9
Library of Congress Catalog Number 2018968302

Printed in the United States of America
Second Printing: 2020

24 23 22 21 20   6 5 4 3 2

Cover Illustration by A Collective
Interior Design & Cover Design by Kim Morehead

Wise Ink Creative Publishing
807 Broadway St. NE, Suite 46
Minneapolis, MN 55413
www.wiseink.com

*For Ella: May you explore the world with
fierce independence and scientific inquiry.*

*For Mya, Eva, and Lia: Find your inspiration.
If you love what you do, you will never work a day in your life.*

*For Carolina, my incredible wife:
Marrying you was the best decision I ever made.*

Table of Contents

Foreword

Everybody needs some help on their journey to becoming the best person they can be. If you watch some of the latest superhero movies, it's not hard to realize a common theme throughout them. Behind every superhero, there's a motivational or inspirational force that helps shape them. Like a super hero, a **STEM mentor** will guide you along your lifelong adventure (**S**cience, **T**echnology, **E**ngineering and **M**ath). STEM mentors can be people you know or others that inspire you: from environmentalists such as Rachel Carson to computer scientists like Margaret Hamilton.

Growing up as a girl in a small town with around only 500 inhabitants, I've had to depend on past and present STEM superheroes to motivate and inspire me to be the best version of myself. My hope for the future is a world where all girls who are interested in STEM will be able to follow the examples set by the smart, successful women who came before them.

I sometimes feel discouraged or wonder about the future ahead of me. When the doubts begin to creep in, I remember to recognize all the amazing women in STEM before me who have made it possible for my STEM goals to be within reach. Their never-ending effort to secure a spot in the world of STEM encourages me to keep trying and never give up. There are no limits to who your role models can be, and you can choose your own based on your interests. This book is full of STEM Superheroes, but they are just the tip of the iceberg. Find someone who is making a difference in the world – from around the corner to around the globe, be inspired and get started on your STEM superhero adventure today!

Grace
Middle School STEM Student
Nezperce, Idaho

Who Are Everyday STEM Superheroes?

Think about your favorite superheroes. What do they look like? What are their superpowers? How do they use these powers to make a difference in their communities? Look around you, and you will find everyday superheroes in this world. These superheroes are the people who work in the areas of science, technology, engineering, and math (STEM). STEM superheroes work in your community, using their superpowers to make your town, country, and world a better place.

STEM professionals are everyday people just like you and me. They have families, pets, friends, and brothers and sisters. They have favorite foods and hobbies like biking, hiking, and having picnics in the park. They also ask lots of questions to understand our world, and they use the answers to change it: they design buildings, build electronics, protect our parks, and much more. The work they do often makes our communities safer, healthier, and cleaner. From your neighborhood pharmacy to the satellites zipping above our atmosphere, STEM superheroes are helping to make the world a better place!

Have you heard of the three trailblazing astronauts Sally Ride, Mae Jemison and Ellen Ochoa? How did the six STEM superpowers get these three amazing women into space? They used all six superpowers to help them blast off. As kids they were **curious** about space, our **solar system**, and the planets. The spaceships they traveled in were built by **collaborative** teams. Read on to explore STEM jobs on Earth and outer space!

ABCDEFGHIJKLMNOPQRSTUVWXYZ

From A to Z, let's find out more about the careers and powers of every-day STEM superheroes!

What Are STEM Superpowers?

Much like comic-book superheroes, STEM professionals possess amazing skills that they use to solve problems and fight for good. There are six STEM superpowers that these superheroes use to make the world a better place. Many of these superheroes developed their powers at school, but super STEM skills can also grow at home and on the job. Unlike in comic books, anyone can have STEM superpowers and be an everyday superhero!

The six STEM superpowers are:

- **Observation:** gathering information using your five senses.

- **Imagination and Curiosity:** wanting to know or learn something and being creative in forming new ideas about what you learn.

- **Problem solving:** finding solutions using creativity, design, and testing.

- **Collaboration:** working together to solve problems.

- **Data Collection and Analysis:** gathering and interpreting information to make informed decisions.

- **Communication:** explaining information to others in clear and simple ways and listening to other ideas.

What STEM Superpowers Do You Have?

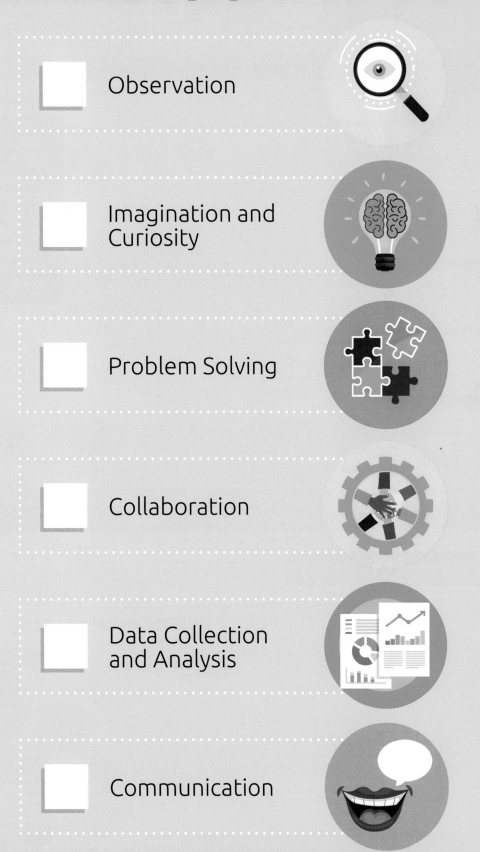

☐ Observation

☐ Imagination and Curiosity

☐ Problem Solving

☐ Collaboration

☐ Data Collection and Analysis

☐ Communication

Observation

Superpowers

 Use your five senses to discover the world around you.

Describe the features of what you see and do!

 Make a record of what you observe by drawing or writing.

 Use your observations to make predictions.

Look around. What do you see? Maybe you live in a city with lots of buildings, roads, and people. Are you on a farm with chickens, goats, and cows? Are you in a small town with only your favorite restaurant and one grocery store? Perhaps you see a beautiful sandy beach and waves constantly crashing just outside the window. What do your observations tell you about the organisms living near you and their habitat? Wherever you live, you can use the **superpower** of observation to explore the world around you. Observing the world helps us stay curious and develop questions to explore. The ability to observe and record observations is an important superpower STEM superheroes use to accomplish their work. You can observe the world around you using your five senses.

Scientific Method

Observation is the first step in the scientific method. Recorded observations are used to make predictions, experiment, and test hypotheses.

Five Senses
— what you

 See

 Think

 Feel

 Hear

 Smell

STEM superheroes gather information by using their five senses or instruments to make observations.

Superwomen Observing

South African naturalist Marjorie Courtenay-Latimer was fishing in 1938 and caught a coelacanth. This fish was thought to have been extinct for more than sixty-five million years. Marjorie's observations are considered a major scientific discovery. She found a living fossil!

Dr. Jane Goodall observed chimpanzees in their natural habitat in Tanzania. She wrote down what she saw, felt, and smelled, and described how the chimps interacted, slept, and ate. Her observations helped to protect the animals' habitat and made her into a well-known conservationist.

Superpower Instruments

Magnifying glass

Microscope

Satellite

Telescope

Ruler

X-ray machine

Thermometer

Pencil

Notebook

Can

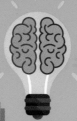

Imagination and Curiosity

Superpowers

 Journal or draw what you think, feel, or imagine.

 Read! Reading will help you think about new places, people, and problems to solve!

 Try to create something every day. Paint. Draw. Sing. Dance. Build.

 Use objects in different ways.

Have you ever thought about the fact that we live on a giant blue ball floating through space? Earth is our spaceship as we travel through the galaxy at amazing speeds.

Each day we invent new technology, discover new forms of life, and explore our planet. Thanks to our **imagination** and **curiosity**, we make discoveries and find ways to improve life on Spaceship Earth. Imagine how objects could be changed or adapted. What new technologies do you imagine will exist in your future? Some of the greatest inventions start with a wild imagination!

> **The ability to think about silly and serious things, ask lots of questions, and have big dreams is the first step to becoming your own STEM superhero.**

Superwomen Imagining and Curious

Robots that have Skin

From vacuuming robots to security at airports, we can now see robots just about anywhere. You may also be familiar with robots you cannot see, but only hear, such as Alexa and Siri. What could new robots look like? The imagination of Dr. Stéphanie Lacour is designing what robot skin might look like. Dr. Lacour wants robot skin to be stretchy and respond to pressure or touch. It could also be used on prosthetic arms and legs. To design it, Dr. Lacour's team asks questions such as:

- **What color should robot skin be?**
- **What should robot skin feel like?**
- **Should the skin look different on different parts of the robot?**
- **What happens to robot skin when it runs into a wall or a door?**

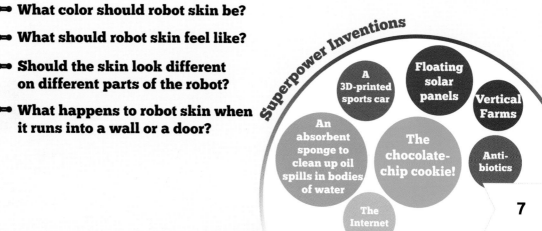

Superpower Inventions

- A 3D-printed sports car
- Floating solar panels
- Vertical Farms
- An absorbent sponge to clean up oil spills in bodies of water
- The chocolate-chip cookie!
- Antibiotics
- The Internet

Problem Solving

Superpowers

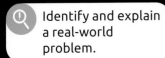
Identify and explain a real-world problem.

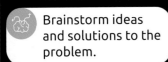
Brainstorm ideas and solutions to the problem.

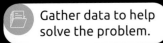
Gather data to help solve the problem.

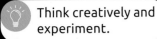
Think creatively and experiment.

Observing the world and asking questions gets STEM superheroes flying. But more than asking the right questions, STEM superheroes have to find problems that can be solved. They could be big problems that affect all of humanity or small problems that affect communities or individuals. Start by asking yourself what needs exist in your home, school, or community. What can you do to help? Once you have a real-world problem to address, it's time to brainstorm solutions, create and test them, and keep trying. You are now doing design thinking to help solve problems!

> **Design thinking is an approach to solving problems that focuses on creativity, testing, and collaborating with your audience to address the problem.**

Superwomen Problem Solvers

Orbital Calculations
Have you seen the movie *Hidden Figures?*

If you have, you may know the names Katherine Coleman Goble Johnson, Mary Jackson, and Dorothy Vaughan. All three mathematicians did critical mathematical calculations for the Redstone, Mercury, and Apollo space programs. Mathematicians played an important role in getting people into space. In fact, without their calculations we wouldn't have been able to send anyone into space safely. We called them human computers because of all of their calculations. Johnson calculated the orbital math equations that led to the success of the first (1962) and subsequent US crewed space flights. Without her calculations, we wouldn't know how to safely land spacecraft.

Superhero Eunice Foote was the first scientist to make the connection between the amount of carbon dioxide in our atmosphere and climate change. She discovered CO_2's warming properties in 1856! Her experiment and findings were presented at the annual meeting of the American Association for the Advancement of Science by Professor Joseph Henry of the Smithsonian Institute. At the time, her findings might have been disregarded because she was a woman and not a member of the association, but she collaborated with a colleague to share her findings.

Superpower in Action

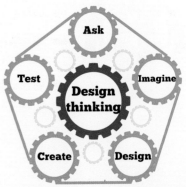

Collaboration

 Work cooperatively as a member of a group.

 Enable critical and creative thinking.

 Make connections and create partnerships.

 Embrace diversity and cultivate inclusion.

Our world is full of amazing people who have different strengths, skills, and interests. When people work together to solve problems, they are collaborating. Remember the three astronauts, Sally Ride, Mae Jemison and Ellen Ochoa? A team of engineers, rocket scientists and safety experts built the rocket and their space suits. The team collaborated to design, build and test these things to keep them safe in space. STEM professionals share their expertise and knowledge to solve problems. Research shows that **collaborating** with people who have different backgrounds increases the strength of the collaboration. Individual STEM professionals may focus on one area, but we need to make discoveries as a team.

> Almost everything you use every day required a team of professionals to design, build, and create. When people work together to solve problems, they are collaborating.

 ## Superwomen Collaborating

In 2018 a group of US high school seniors collaborated to encourage students to act on climate change. More than 250 students across the United States dedicated sixty seconds of their speeches to encouraging other students to take action on climate change. Talk about power! This collaboration was led by Potential Energy, a coalition of nonprofits and organizations dedicated to addressing climate change.

The first house in the US with solar panels was built by two women. In 1948, Dr. Maria Telkes, an architect or builder, and Eleanor Raymond, collaborated. The house was built in Massachusetts. The team proved that the sun could power a house even in a cold climate!

Superpower Actions

Shared goals

Creative atmosphere

Reading

Thinking

Commitment to participate

Listening

Data Collection and Analysis

 Gather relevant data from multiple sources.

 Recognize cause-and-effect relationships.

 Analyze data.

 Draw conclusions from data.

From the number of 'likes' on your social media to sports team scores, there are a lot of data in our world. It's everywhere! We collect data through observation, asking questions, and taking measurements. We don't want to use old data. We don't make decisions based on our thoughts or feelings alone. We learn from reading, communicating, and imagining. We use data to understand our world and make decisions. What data do you use?

> *Data* is defined as a collection of related facts or figures (numbers). *Datum* refers to a single item of factual information.

⭐ Superwomen Data Driven Decision Makers

The US military trains worldwide, from remote deserts to computer labs. Bohemia Interactive Simulations leader Eva Saravia creates simulation programs to train soldiers using real data and simulated objects. Her online trainings include such situations as wrecked cars, small villages, and signs in the language of the training location. All these data help our military be ready for the real world.

Do you like bugs? Some of them can ruin food or damage homes, so humans invented pesticides to keep bugs away. In the 1950s many American families used a pesticide called DDT. We thought it was helping us, but the data collected by scientist Rachel Carson told us otherwise. DDT was harming crops, wildlife, and humans. Today, based on her research, we have banned the use of DDT.

Superpower Questions

⁇ Where does the data come from?

⁇ Who collected the data?

⁇ How old is the data?

⁇ What is the **mean, median,** or **mode** of the data?

Communication

Superpowers

 Introduce the topic.

 Check for understanding by asking questions.

 Share your predictions, inventions and conclusions.

 Use visuals to make a call to action.

Think about the great stories of superwomen you have already read. Many of them worked hard to tell the world about why their work is important and how others can use it. **Communicating** about STEM inventions, findings, and discoveries is key. We can communicate in a variety of ways, from talking to posting in social media to writing books, and more. Communication is also key to collaboration. When we collaborate, we have to be able to explain what we are doing. We cannot solve a problem without communicating clearly with others on our team and listening carefully to their explanations as well.

Communication in STEM is the ability to take specific knowledge and explain it to others in clear and understandable ways.

 ## Superwomen Communicators

Do you want to communicate scientific findings? Meet Nicole Hernandez Hammer, a sea-level scientist and environmental activist. In addition to doing research, she makes sure that her findings are known in communities. Her work focuses on helping the Latinx community understand how climate change negatively affects them. She educates and mobilizes people to advocate, protest, and vote.

Are you good at talking or writing? You may want to follow in the footsteps of Dr. Sheila Ochugboju, an international science communicator! She is an expert in biochemistry. She travels across Europe and Africa, talking about science and technology.

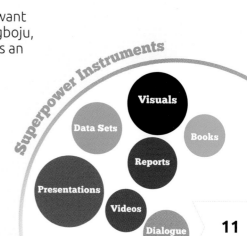

Superpower Instruments

Visuals
Data Sets
Books
Reports
Presentations
Videos
Dialogue

The STEM Superpowers

Developing your STEM superpowers will help you accomplish your goals. Many of the superpowers are already within you, waiting to be used. Others can be learned and strengthened every day! Do you have a dream of going to space? Do you imagine discovering a new species? Are you curious about the world around you? Do you have a problem you want to solve? Do you communicate and collaborate with your classmates? These are your STEM superpowers!

As you read the profiles of everyday STEM superheroes, remember that these professionals were once students just like you. They worked hard in school and at home to develop their STEM superpowers. Learn about them. Explore beyond this book to learn more.

 Draw or write about the STEM Superpowers you have or want.

Discover STEM

Look for these icons in the book.

 Meet STEM superheroes from the past and present.

 Meet some of the first STEM Superheroes.

 Learn new facts.

 Use your STEM superpowers to take action.

 Problem solve with these think-and-discuss questions.

Where Can We Find Everyday Superheroes?

ABCDEFGHIJKLMNOPQRSTUVWXYZ

Above the Earth

Look up at the night sky. Do you see the planet Venus, Mars, Jupiter, or Saturn? How many stars can you see? The starlight you see has traveled through space for thousands or even millions of years to reach your eyes tonight. You are looking into the past.

Astronomers explore the night sky using **telescopes**. Some telescopes are based on land, while others orbit Earth on satellites. Astronomers observe the universe and collect data and details about our solar system and beyond. They help us search for exoplanets, which are planets that orbit other stars in the Milky Way galaxy, our galaxy. More than two thousand exoplanets have been discovered by astronomers using the Kepler space-based X-ray telescope. In fact, astronomer Sara Seager led the discovery of more than seven hundred exoplanets!

Did you know that astronomers can use more than visible light to explore the cosmos? Visible light—the light humans can see with their eyes—is only a small section of a much larger electromagnetic spectrum. The full spectrum includes radio waves, microwaves, X-rays, and gamma rays. In the twentieth century, astronomers developed radio telescopes, such as the Atacama Large Array in Chile and the Arecibo Observatory in Puerto Rico, to capture and analyze radio waves in space. These telescopes detect radio waves emitted by stars, black holes, and supernovas, data that can tell us how fast stars are spinning and other fascinating details of our universe.

Four nuns—Emila Ponzoni, Regina Colombo, Concetta Finardi and Luigia Panceri—helped to create the first map of the stars between 1887 and 1889. By mapping and measuring nearly a half a million stars' positions in the sky, their research would be used to create the first celestial map.

Dr. Wanda Diaz Merced

Dr. Merced is an astronomer who studies gamma-ray bursts. Dr. Merced lost her sight late in life due to illness. However, she continues to observe stars by collecting data as sound files. When she could no longer see the data on supernovas and solar flares collected by her scientific instruments, Dr. Merced invented a technique to turn her data into sound files. She called this new process sonification. Other astronomers realized that sonification allowed them to recognize patterns in the data that they might not have previously noticed. Dr. Merced's superpowers of creativity and imagination not only helped her to analyze data, but also showed how people can succeed despite limits.

Building a Green City

Think about your city or town. How safe is the area where you ride a bike? Is it dangerous? Can you ride your bicycle into the city center easily, or do you have to cross lots of traffic? What would you change to help make your city safe for bicyclists? How about for people on foot, or pedestrians? What other improvements can you imagine for your town or city?

Civil engineers are superheroes who design or redesign the form and feel of a city. They help to plan roads, buildings, dams, bridges, airports, and other big projects. Most civil engineers can be found at construction sites, collaborating with other STEM professionals. They also work with city officials, such as mayors, councils, and chief sustainability directors, to consider questions such as: How can we protect the city center from flooding? How can we reduce the number of traffic accidents? Where can we create new green spaces for the community to enjoy?

Many cities around the world were designed in the twentieth century to allow cars and trucks to easily move through them. Today, civil engineers are working to create more green spaces in city centers. In Europe, they are turning streets built for cars into zones for walking and bicycling. In Barcelona, Spain, civil engineers are creating large, car-free areas called "superblocks." These superblocks are for pedestrians and bikes only and reduce **pollution** while creating more space for citizens. Do you have a place like this in your community?

Use your STEM journal to draw, sketch, or paint a city that is friendly to the **environment**. Imagine green spaces, bike paths, animal homes, and fun places to play.

A B . . . . Z

Vanessa Galvez

After a big rainstorm, have you ever wondered where all the dirty water running down the streets goes? Vanessa Galvez is a civil engineer who uses her STEM superpower of problem solving to design solutions for storm water. Storm water is full of pollution. To prevent it from getting into nearby rivers and lakes, or the ocean, Galvez designs and creates bioswales. Bioswales are areas of water-absorbing plants and soil. The roots of the plants capture the pollutants, which are then broken down by bacteria in the soil. Galvez constructs bioswales near sidewalks and streets, and in other areas where runoff and storm water are collected before entering a stream or river. Many of them add beauty to the neighborhood as well as protecting bodies of water.

Chasing Storms

METEOROLOGIST

Can you **predict** the future? How cool would it be to know what would happen three or ten days in advance? If you watch TV, you probably have seen a weather person, or **meteorologist**, predict the path of a hurricane or blizzard. How do they see into the future? By using the STEM superpower of data collection and analysis, meteorologists create a forecast, or informed projection, of what the weather will be. Meteorologists study Earth's atmosphere to help us understand our weather and **climate**. Some examples of the data they collect are:

- **temperature**: how hot or cold the air is

- **precipitation**: how much water is falling from the sky as rain, snow, sleet, or hail

- air pressure: how much the atmosphere presses down on Earth's surface

- wind patterns: patterns of wind across the hemispheres

Meteorologists collect these data points and use them to forecast the weather. We use these forecasts to plan our vacations, sports events, and birthday parties. They help us prepare for changes in our environment, such as ice on roads or snow at a ski resort. Meteorologists also save lives by alerting the public to weather disasters, such as tornadoes, hurricanes, and blizzards.

 Meteorologists use a variety of tools to collect data. From giant weather balloons in the sky to satellites in outer space to buoys in the ocean, data about temperature and air pressure is collected. This data is used to create maps and charts showing the patterns of weather!

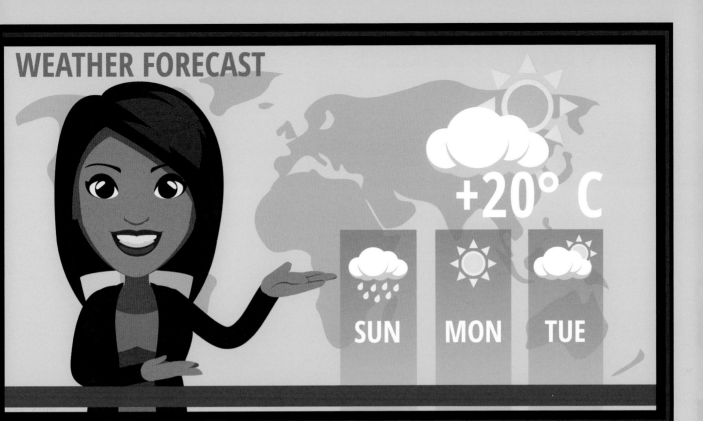

WEATHER FORECAST

+20° C

SUN   MON   TUE

SUPERHERO

Brittney Shipp

Meteorologists work for the military and the government, and most commonly for TV or radio stations. Brittney Shipp is an award-winning meteorologist who uses her data analysis and communication superpowers to ensure the Philadelphia area has **accurate** weather forecasts. Shipp loves to communicate the weather on TV; she has reported on dust storms, tornadoes, blizzards, and everything in between. Shipp's dream of being a TV meteorologist began when she was a kid and got curious about the weather. She uses her STEM super power of communication to encourage kids so they can pursue their own STEM superhero dreams. Shipp makes many school visits, speaking to kids to help them understand weather and the many science-related careers. She even wrote a children's book, *The Meteorologist in Me,* to remind us that we can do anything if we put our minds to it.

Driving on Mars

ROBOTICS ENGINEER

Can you imagine controlling a full-size robot car on another planet? If you could create a robot, what planet would you explore with it? What would you name your robot?

Robotics is an area of technology that focuses on machines designed to perform precise functions or actions. We use robots across many areas of life: medicine, construction, environmental sciences, automobile engineering, space exploration, and much more. Some robots are controlled by people, while others can be programmed to carry out commands on their own. Some robots look and move like people, but many more do not. Scientists and engineers continually research new designs, materials, and methods for engineering robots.

What will robots look like in the year 2050? What kinds of things that you do now will be done by robots and other machines?

One of the biggest space mysteries was recently solved by a robot on Mars—139 million miles away from Earth! A team of engineers, rocket scientists, and astronauts collaborated to design, build, test, and land a robot named Curiosity on the surface of Mars. In 2011, Curiosity began its journey from Earth to Mars. It weighs more than 8,500 pounds. Imagine how much math, science, engineering, and technology it took to land it successfully on another planet! Today, Curiosity is controlled by scientists and engineers on Earth. It uses cameras and sensors of different types to collect data about the planet's surface. This information is sent back to the National Aeronautics and Space Administration (NASA) for analysis by scientists and mathematicians. In 2015, Curiosity found evidence of liquid water on Mars. This is an important clue to how life developed in our solar system! Curiosity is still discovering and collecting data from the red planet today.

Valentina Tereshkova was the first woman on Earth to go into outer space. She also was the first woman to fly solo, or alone, on a space mission. As an astronaut, she spent three days in space and went around the Earth 48 times in 1963. She was from the former Soviet Union, now present-day Russia.

A··D············Z

Dr. Vandi Verma

Dr. Verma is a robotics engineer at NASA and one of Curiosity's main drivers. Dr. Verma uses her math skills to program and send hundreds of computer commands and calculations to Curiosity. The calculations tell the robot where to go, how fast to go, what pictures of the planet to take, and where and when to collect soil and rock samples. These pictures and samples are used by scientists at NASA to understand more about Mars. What happens if there is a dust storm or Curiosity gets stuck in a crater? Dr. Verma uses her problem-solving skills to resend or change the commands. Dr. Verma uses her superpowers of collaboration and problem solving to help us understand our solar system.

Exploring Earth's History

GEOLOGIST

How old are you? How old is that tree in your front yard? How old is the sand in the sandbox? How old is Earth? A million years may seem like a long time, but **geologists** have determined that Earth is approximately four billion, six hundred million (4,600,000,000) years old.

To understand how old Earth is, geologists collect and study data from Earth's crust, rocks on the moon, and meteorites. This study of rocks and **minerals** is called geology (*geo* means "earth" in Latin, and *-ology* means "the study of"). Their studies take them all over the world—from the coldest places on Earth, such as Antarctica, to the hottest, such as Death Valley, California—to find answers to questions about our planet's history. They use their superpowers of imagination and curiosity to ask interesting questions about our home planet and then use their data-collection skills to answer those questions.

Ursula Bailey was a planetary geologist who studied meteorites in Antarctica and analyzed moon rocks collected by the Apollo moon missions.

Rocks tell a story about the past, present, and future of a planet. Rocks on Earth might hold **fossils** of plants and animals that tell us about life in the past. Rocks are made of minerals such as iron, gold, tin, copper, and lead. These minerals are needed to make useful everyday objects. From the bricks in your school's walls to the battery that runs an electric car, rocks and minerals are needed to produce much of what we use every day. Geologists work daily to understand Earth's history and find the resources we need to build communication networks, manufacture cars and trucks, and construct shelters and public spaces in our communities.

Make observations in your house and identify items that may be made from rocks or minerals. **Record** your observations and then use a computer to research what everyday items are made with rocks and minerals.

A···E·············Z

Dr. Gabriela Farfan

A childhood love for rocks led Dr. Farfan to seek a doctoral degree (PhD) in marine chemistry and geochemistry. As part of her degree program, she studied rocks and oceanography at the Massachusetts Institute of Technology. Dr. Farfan used her superpower of data analysis to understand the minerals found in coral reefs. Dr. Farfan's research helps us understand how to protect coral reefs. Today, with her doctorate degree in hand, you will find Dr. Farfan as a curator in the Smithsonian National Museum of Natural History in Washington, DC. Dr. Farfan will be working with the world's largest collections of gems (10,000) and minerals (350,000) in the National Gem and Mineral Collection. Dr. Farfan will use her superpowers of communication to help museum goers learn about the amazing collection and collaborate with geologists to understand its history and importance in today's world.

Feeding a Nation

VERTICAL FARMER

Did you ever stop to think about how much food is needed to feed a nation? Think about how much food you eat in a year. Then multiply that by 300 million people in the United States or 7 billion people in the world. That's a lot of hungry people!

Humans have grown plants for food for thousands of years. Farming has changed dramatically over the centuries, from using hands and tools to plant crops, to using animals to help till the dirt, to using giant tractors to manage enormous farms. Traditional agriculture requires lots of land, but technology is reshaping where and how we farm.

Can you farm inside? Yes! You can visit the largest **vertical farm** in Massachusetts to see how. Vertical farms such as this one grow produce, or vegetables and fruits, in giant warehouses, even in the middle of the city. Instead of growing in big, flat fields, the plants grow on shelves or stacks. This saves a lot of space and also conserves water and soil. Some vertical farms use sunlight, while others have LED lights that shine on plants twenty-four hours a day. Some plants in vertical farms don't even need soil to grow! Indoor vertical farming allows produce to be grown year-round in places that might not have the space or the environment to grow food.

What regions of the world would benefit most from vertical farming? Think about the distance that food travels from farm to table. This distance is called food miles.

Today, there are nearly a million women farmers in the US. These farmers plant, harvest, fix fences or planters, and even deliver baby animals.

A····F·········Z

Sonia Lo

Sonia Lo is the Chief Executive Officer of Crop One Holdings, the biggest vertical farm in the world. She combines her business skills and love of food with science to grow environmentally friendly foods. Growing food uses a lot of water. In fact, over 70 percent of the water used today helps to grow food. Crop One saves over 90 percent of the water that traditional farming uses, grows green produce for over 38 supermarkets in Massachusetts, and will be growing for a major airline in Dubai. Massachusetts is known for cold winters with many blizzards and a short growing season. Imagine growing fresh lettuce, kale, and spinach in the middle of winter! Dubai is in the middle of a desert and they will still have fresh produce year-round. This advancement in farming not only saves water but also provides fresh produce to communities all year long.

Greening Our Energy

RENEWABLE ENERGY FINANCIAL ANALYST

How much does electricity cost? Did you know that each time you leave a light or computer on when not using it, you are throwing away money and wasting energy? Knowing where your **energy** comes from helps you use it responsibly.

For any business to succeed, someone has to be responsible for keeping track of money and cost. Energy costs money because we need to build and maintain power sources to generate and deliver it. In some places, electricity comes from burning **fossil fuels**, such as coal or natural gas. Environmentally friendly energy, which is often called green energy, comes from sources such as wind, water, the sun, and Earth's own internal, or geothermal, heat.

To find out how much each kind of energy costs, we rely on **financial analysts**. These professionals use their math skills and complex formulas, data tables, and computers to help track the costs of power. Financial analysts use data to help power companies, cities, and individuals make decisions about energy.

Financial analysts in the field of **renewable energy** help make the world a greener place. When someone wants to build a new renewable energy project, such as a solar or wind farm, financial analysts figure out how long construction will take, what it will cost, and how much money and energy these projects will create. This information also helps businesses and cities to decide if and where a new green energy project will happen.

We think of farms as places that grow food. What about a solar or a wind farm? These large energy projects are found in the US. Draw a picture of a solar or wind farm.

The first home with solar panels in the United States was built in 1948 in Massachusetts by two superheroes, Dr. Maria Telkes and architect Eleanor Raymond. Dr. Telkes was known as the "Sun Queen" for all her solar-powered inventions.

A ····· G ········ ········· Z

Hannah Olmberg-Soesman

An energy operator and award-winning renewable energy analyst, Hannah Olmberg-Soesman is using the power of the sun to help communities in her home country, Suriname. Located on the northern coast of South America, Suriname has lots of sunshine, but most of its electricity comes from burning fossil fuels. These energy sources are expensive for families and harmful for the country. Olmberg-Soesman is collaborating with local power companies and communities to develop solar projects that solve this problem. She assesses the costs and savings for solar projects and then helps communities finance and install them.

Helping Us Understand Our Bodies

BIOMEDICAL ENGINEER

How can a cookie or gummy bear allow doctors to gather data about sick children? Tiny sensors placed in a tasty treat can allow doctors to collect data about a patient's digestive **system**!

Biomedical engineers combine engineering principles with medical sciences to design and create equipment, devices, computer systems, and software used in healthcare. Many of them work in manufacturing, where they invent tools to gather data on everyday human activities, such as eating, walking, and sleeping. These tools might be tiny sensors, like those used to diagnose digestive illnesses, or wearable devices, such as fitness trackers. Data collection is a big part of all STEM professions. Today, rapid advancements in **biometric** devices are helping to gather and analyze more data about human health than ever before.

The Fitbit®, for example, can track sleep patterns, steps taken, heartbeat, and much more. Biomedical engineers are designing new biomedical technologies that can travel through our bodies to provide data on internal organs and body systems without the need for surgery.

The 30-Day Jumping Jack Challenge is an app to track jumping jacks over the course of thirty days. This app lets you act like a scientist by gathering data about your physical activity and creating graphs to show your progress. If you could design an app that uses biometric data to reach a physical activity goal, what app would you design?

A ⋯⋯ H ⋯⋯⋯⋯⋯⋯ Z

Dr. Jayanthi Narasimhan

The older we get, the harder it is to stay healthy, yet your grandparents may forget to take their medicine or accidentally miss a doctor's appointment. Smartphones can remind us of important things, but it's easy to forget them, too. Dr. Narasimhan used her superpowers of imagination and problem solving to create a wearable technology that helps track data for the elderly. Dr. Narasimhan designed an interactive watch, the WatchRx, that solves multiple problems. Its apps remind wearers to take medication or go to the doctor. It collects and tracks biometric data, such as heartbeat and steps, to help wearers get the right amount of exercise. It has tools to help people who get lost easily or need help finding doctors' offices. It even has a phone! WatchRx is a technology not just for aging grandparents, but also for their caregivers. Doctors can monitor data from the WatchRx on an app developed for mobile devices. Dr. Narasimhan continues to make improvements to the WatchRx, which makes life better for more people each day.

31

Innovative Learning

VIRTUAL-WORLD CREATOR

Have you ever wondered what it would be like to walk on the moon, visit the Taj Mahal, or walk through the Amazon rainforest? Wouldn't it be cool to explore these places from the comfort of your classroom or living room?

Virtual reality (VR) allows you to use visual headsets to explore three-dimensional environments created on computers. Everyday STEM superheroes use their imagination and technology skills to turn data into incredibly realistic visual environments. VR is also used to train other everyday STEM superheroes. Fighter pilots in the navy, doctors in medical school, and aircraft mechanics all use VR to improve their professional skills in a safe environment before experiencing the real thing.

In the classroom, you can now explore distant planets or the ocean depths of our own planet using VR! The British Broadcasting Company (BBC) created a program called Earth that lets students explore as scuba divers swimming along the California coast or a sea otter living in the Pacific Ocean. This program brings the underwater experience to classrooms that cannot visit the ocean. Students can even see some of the smallest creatures in the ocean, **zooplankton**.

What problem could we solve with VR? Think of a problem and draw a picture of the solution in your VR world.

Helen Situ

Imagine sitting in the front row, watching your favorite team compete for the WNBA championship. You can see all your favorite players' faces. You can hear the loud cheers of the crowd as a free throw swishes through the basket. VR is now extending into sports! Helen Situ is a virtual-world creator who began her career reimagining and designing VR sports arenas. She recreates the colors of the seats and courts, the brightness of the lights, the location of scoreboards, and the size of the arena. Her passion for virtual reality extends into her virtual publication, *Virtual Reality Pop*, which communicates happenings in the VR world. Today, she is the Chief Executive Officer and cofounder of Moment, a 3D technology tool to help VR creators bring their worlds to life!

Jumping for Data

APPLICATION DEVELOPER

Do you play games on a smartphone or tablet? Do you have an app that lets you edit your photos, or one that tracks your steps or heart rate? Using the superpowers of creativity and data analysis, app developers design mobile applications to help us get organized, track fitness, connect with friends, and much more.

App developers design, code, test, and launch mobile apps for a huge variety of needs. An important skill for this career is coding. Coding is like a recipe: specific lines of instruction add up to make the app function. There are many different coding languages. One of the first programming languages for computers, COBOL, was developed by an awesome STEM superhero, Navy Rear Admiral Grace Brewster Murray Hopper.

Other coding languages include:

- SQL
- Python
- PHP
- Java and JavaScript
- C, C#, or C++

You may be most familiar with the game, map, or messaging apps on your phone, but apps also run smart televisions, online banking, and car navigation systems. App developers can help thousands or even millions of people simplify their lives so they can spend more time with their families.

Have you played Minecraft®? It's a learning game designed for you to actively solve problems. Learners are able to design and build cities, collaborate with others, and record data.

A········J····· ·········z

Lyndsey Scott

Lyndsey Scott has two identities: fashion model and app developer. Her passion for coding began at the age of twelve. Scott has written games for the TI-89 graphing calculator, iPhones, and iPads. She earned a theater and computer science degree and today codes in five languages (Python, C++, Java, MIPS, and Objective-C). Scott uses her superpower of communication to help kids get into coding with online classes. She works to create a world where coding is for everyone!

Knocking on the Door of 3D Worlds

3D ANIMATOR

Have you ever been to a three-dimensional (3D) movie where you had to wear special glasses? Do you love feeling like a shark is swimming right up to your nose or as if you were zipping through a roller coaster? Welcome to the world of **3D animation**!

3D animation is about making objects in movies, video games, television shows, and even commercials seem to move beyond the screen. To create these animations, you need to combine your superpower of imagination with computer animation software skills. The software allows animators to create many images that are put together to form a 3D world. Many 3D animators focus on a specific area of animation, such as characters, scenery, or background design.

Before any animation begins, there must be a story. Animators work with writers, actors, and app developers to bring a script together with art and technology. Using their superpowers of collaboration and communication, 3D animators ensure that their animations reflect the story that writers and directors want to tell.

In two-dimensional (2D) animation, such as old cartoon shows, images are drawn by hand. For 3D animation, computer software is used to create images. Why is the process different?

A·······•·····**K**·····•····•·······Z

Sonya Carey

Sonya Carey is an animator of both 2D and 3D films. She uses her STEM superpower of imagination to create characters for movies and TV series. As an animator, she uses both hand-drawn and computer-generated images to create movie characters. She imagines what the characters look like, what they wear, and what emotions they feel. She reads the writers' scripts and listens carefully to the actors as they record characters' voices. Then, to bring the stories to life, she collaborates with a team of STEM professionals. She created Disney's first African American princess, Tiana, for *The Princess and the Frog* (2009). She also worked on the 2011 film *Winnie the Pooh*.

Launching Satellites

Have you ever watched a rocket launch? Google it. They are awesome! Did you know that rockets often carry cargo that is then released into orbit around our planet? These objects that orbit our planet and others are called satellites.

Aerospace engineers design and build rockets and the satellites they carry. They use their advanced math skills to calculate how much force and speed rockets need to launch into space. Working with astronauts, physicists, and electrical engineers, they design, build, and test the machines that explore and connect our planet.

Satellites orbiting Earth, the moon, and other objects in the solar system gather and transmit data. Satellites around Earth transmit our TV and cell phone signals, track the weather, and direct map apps. Other satellites gather data to help STEM professionals understand our solar system: some take pictures of the surface of Earth and other planets, while others collect data about gravity on the moon, radiation on Mars, and much more. The work of aerospace engineers is critical in observing and understanding our Earth and the universe beyond.

Want to launch your own satellite into space?
Beginning in fifth grade, STEM superheroes just like you can send mini satellites into space through the Student Spaceflight Experiments Program. Teams of student STEM superheroes have sent hundreds of mini satellite packages into space.

Imagine and draw a satellite for your community in your STEM journal. What data would your satellite collect? How could the satellite help your community?

Dr. Danielle Wood

Dr. Wood uses the same superpowers of observation and curiosity today as she did when she was a child in Florida, watching space shuttle launches. Today, she is an aerospace engineer, professor, and founder of Space Enabled. Through Space Enabled, Dr. Wood leads scientists, engineers, and policy makers in collaboration to fund, design, build, and launch miniaturized satellites. These satellites are smaller than most satellites (about the size of a refrigerator). Dr. Wood's innovation is to build using parts that can be mixed and matched, making satellites cost less. Dr. Wood's innovation allows more communities around the world to be able to create and launch satellites of their own.

Mapping the World

CARTOGRAPHER

Have you ever used a paper map to get somewhere? Do you use an electronic map on your cell phone? Maps help us find the nearest grocery store, a neighborhood park, or the best way to travel long distances when on vacation.

Map Features
- A title tells you what the map is showing.
- A compass rose tells you the directions (north, south, east, and west).
- A bar scale tells you how the map measurements relate to real distances.
- A legend, or key, explains the symbols used on the map.

For thousands of years people used the stars, compasses, and written maps to get from one location to the next. But maps can tell stories too. Maps changed as new technology developed. In the late nineteenth century, four nuns from the Vatican, Emilia Ponzoni, Regina Colombo, Concetta Finardi, and Luigia Panceri, helped to create the first photographic celestial map pinpointing the exact location of every light in the night sky. Much of the world still relies on the ancient technique of reading paper maps today.

Modern-day **cartographers**, or mapmakers, use enormous amounts of data to create electronic maps. Electronic maps use the **Global Positioning System (GPS)**, which allows electronic devices such as cell phones and tablets to pinpoint an exact location. But maps can do much more than help us find places. Cartographers can map air pollution levels over time or plot the migration routes of animals. For example, marine biologists and cartographers used their STEM superpower of collaboration to map the route of humpback whales on their annual five-thousand-kilometer journey from Alaska to Hawaii. Together they discovered that on this long trip the whales sing for up to twenty minutes at a time and repeat the song for hours. Now they are trying to understand why whales sing while migrating. Collaboration with other STEM professionals helps cartographers to imagine new maps to inform our understanding of the world.

Gladys Mae West is a trailblazing mathematician known for her calculations that created the underpinning of the Global Positioning System. She was a mathematician at the US Naval Weapons Laboratory, hired in 1956. At 87 years old, her groundbreaking accomplishments are being recognized nationwide: Gladys West will receive the United States Air Force Space and Missile Pioneers Award.

a·········M·······z

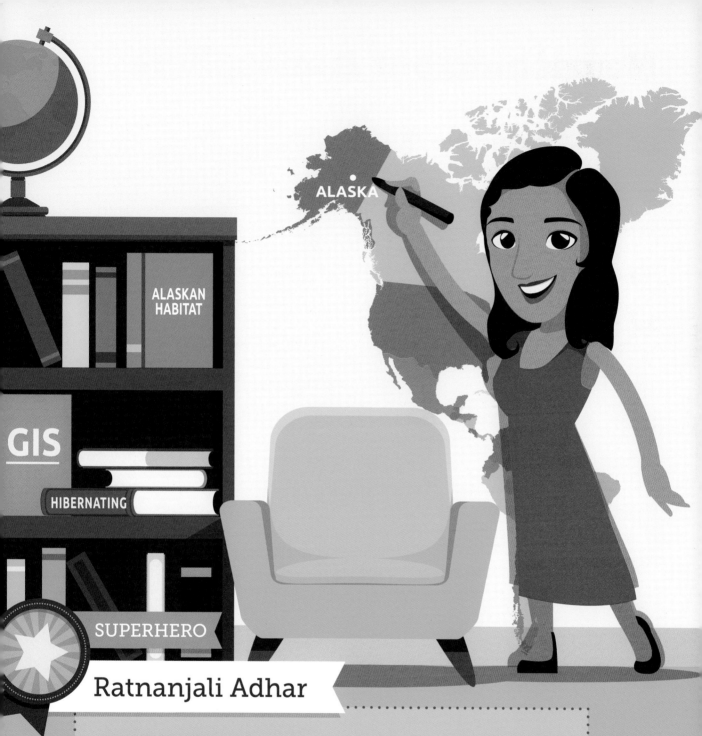

ALASKA

ALASKAN HABITAT

GIS

HIBERNATING

SUPERHERO

Ratnanjali Adhar

Ratnanjali Adhar is an environmental scientist and cartographer. Adhar combines her superpowers of observation and data analysis with her love of wildlife by creating maps that help us to protect the environment. Adhar collects detailed data about the location and environment of different animals to create maps of wildlife **habitats**. Adhar has mapped the location of critically endangered birds for the US Forest Service and wildlife corridors for the National Park Service. Park Rangers and wildlife conservationists use these maps to make informed decisions about how to protect the animals and alert the public about their endangered habitats.

Nourishing our Atmosphere

PARK RANGERS

What element do humans breathe in that plants breathe out? Oxygen. This gas is critical to life on Earth. But where do we get oxygen? Most of us know that plants breathe out oxygen as part of photosynthesis. Forests produce more than half of the oxygen on Earth. Without forests, most life on Earth would likely be single-celled organisms.

To protect our wild, open, and beautiful forests, we need foresters and park rangers. In the United States, we have 58 national parks and more than 10,200 state parks. Rangers and foresters protect not only the forests, but also our mountains, rivers, beaches, and other lands. Park rangers work at local, regional, state, and national parks. To become a park ranger or forester, people study biology, conservation, environmental management, and ecology.

Smokey Bear is our nation's most well-known forester. The famous image was first used in 1947 with the saying, "Only you can prevent forest fires." Like Smokey Bear, park rangers help communicate safety messages and interesting facts about our forests and how to care for them.

The other organism that produces large amounts of Earth's oxygen is a single-celled phytoplankton. Phytoplankton in our oceans produce almost as much oxygen as the world's forests combined.

A·····•••····•N········•···z

Fran Mainella, Claire Marie Hodges, Betty Reid Soskin, and Mary Jane Coltor

These superheroes are some of the first female leaders and protectors of our national parks. In 1918, Claire Marie Hodges became the first woman park ranger, working at Yosemite National Park in California. Mary Jane Colter was an architect who designed four buildings in Grand Canyon National Park: Hermit's Rest (1914), Desert View Watchtower (1932), Lookout Studio (1914), and Hopi House (1905). Fran Mainella was the first woman to serve as director of the National Park Service (2001–2006). At age ninety-six, Betty Reid Soskin became the oldest park ranger in the United States, working at Rosie the Riveter/World War II Home Front National Historical Park in Richmond, California. Each of these leaders used all six of their STEM superpowers!

Opportunities to Save

WEATHERIZATION TECHNICIANS

Do your parents yell at you to turn off the lights? Do you forget to unplug your electronics? We waste massive amounts of energy every day. What can we do about all that wasted energy? Helping communities save energy is the job of a weatherization technician.

Weatherization technicians use their superpower of data analysis to understand the current energy use in buildings. After reviewing this data, they develop a plan to save energy by protecting buildings from the outside elements, reducing electricity usage from lighting, heating, and cooling.

Tips for Weatherizing

- Install energy-saving light bulbs.
- Replace or repair heating systems.
- Update appliances.
- Update windows or window seals.
- Insulate attics, walls, and floors.

Weatherization technologies are helping people understand and save energy. Thermostats are now digital and wireless, allowing people to control the temperature in the house from a phone. Smart switches in homes and businesses help to conserve energy by automatically turning off lights when people leave the room. LED light bulbs use 90 percent less energy. Weatherizing homes, businesses, and schools saves money and uses less energy, which is good for the environment as well.

Does your school have energy **efficiency** goals? Ask your teacher or principal if you can form a team of students to collect data on school energy **consumption**. Use the data to come up with ideas for weatherizing the school or simply changing the energy using behaviors of the teachers and students in your school. Include in your plan what you could do with all the money the school will save by weatherizing the building. Consider joining the US Department of Energy's weatherization competition, the Better Buildings Challenge. This program challenges cities, states, schools, and businesses to weatherize and save energy.

A·····•·••···O········•·z

Jean Diggs

Jean Diggs learned about weatherization on the job as one of the founders of the federal government's Weatherization Assistance Program (WAP). For over forty years, she used her superpower of communication to help people improve their homes and lives. From writing the first set of program regulations to presenting new rules and tips to grantees, she provided the weatherization data that communities needed to solve problems. Diggs spent most of her career at the Department of Energy and retired in 2011. Today, the Jean Diggs WAP Champion Award is given to individuals who are true champions of weatherization.

Protecting the Environment

Have you ever gone swimming in a river or a lake? Do you like to swim in the ocean? Since the 1970s, environmental lawyers have been fighting air and water pollution. You can be a STEM superhero helping to strengthen the laws to make our air and water safer for everyone.

Environmental lawyers work to enforce the laws that regulate the **impact** of human activities on the environment. Environmental law covers a broad range of activities that affect air, water, land, plants, and animals. Environmental lawyers may study science, environmental studies, or economics as well as law. The Clean Water Act, Clean Air Act, and other laws help to protect human health and the environment by enforcing and reducing pollution created by industry and business.

As STEM superheroes, environmental lawyers' strongest superpowers are communication and collaboration. They work with STEM experts to find data and gain expertise about things that damage the environment. Then they communicate that information clearly to help jurors and judges understand how human activities affect our world. They convince others of the importance of protecting our planet.

Much of the world uses coal to power homes and businesses. Coal can be found in West Virginia, North Dakota, Wyoming, and many other places around the world. In West Virginia, coal companies sometimes remove entire mountaintops to reach layers of coal. This practice is harmful in many ways, affecting wildlife, forests, and local streams and rivers. Environmental lawyers have helped to stop the practice of mountaintop removal by researching the scientific data on its effects and communicating them in court.

STEM Superheroes are kids just like you! A collaborating team of kids and young adults filed a lawsuit (Juliana v. United States) against the federal government and oil industry executives. The lawsuit states that the government and private energy companies failed to stop climate change and carbon pollution.

Tara Houska

A lawyer and an **activist**, Tara Houska directs the campaigns and is a Federal Indian Law attorney for the organization Honor the Earth. Honor the Earth is a Native-led activist organization focusing on environmental issues such as the building of oil pipelines and highways that affect communities. As an environmental lawyer and a Native person (Anishinaabe or Ojibwe), she focuses on monitoring and enforcing environmental laws in collaboration with scientists, environmental experts, and Native American communities. She spends her time filing lawsuits to stop construction that threatens the environment and meeting with other people who want to protect Earth.

Questioning Our Footprint

Have you ever seen your footprint in the sand? Your footprint is the mark you made as you stepped along the beach. Footprints can also be a metaphor for bigger changes. Human activity leaves many different marks on the natural world. A footprint on the beach will wash away in the waves, but what about the trees cut down to make paper? What about the coral reefs damaged by commercial fishing?

The impact of society and human activity on their environment is called an **ecological footprint**. This metaphorical footprint includes the waste or trash produced by the people who live there, their energy consumption, and how they use natural resources.

Directors of sustainability measure the environmental and carbon footprint of companies. They look for ways that businesses can have less impact on their neighborhoods and the environment. Directors of sustainability begin by using their STEM superpower of observation to identify the areas that are affected. They then gather data to measure the impact of the project and design plans to reduce its footprint. They might examine how nearby forests, plants, soil, and other natural resources would be affected by new construction. They may even recommend new rules and policies for how new buildings are designed and constructed. They often collaborate with environmental lawyers to make sure that companies follow environmental laws.

What are some of the largest human-made structures you have seen? Discuss the impact they have on the local environment. Think about the materials needed to build the structures and what the land looks like before and after. Here is one example to get you started: The Hoover Dam on the Colorado River just outside Las Vegas, Nevada, generates electricity for a million homes, but the dam stops the natural flow of water. What are some of the impacts of the dam on the river?

Janice Lao

Janice Lao is an environmental scientist with a mind for business. She leads sustainability efforts for hotels in Asia, North America, and Europe. Hotels take up lots of land and create enormous amounts of waste, and hotel visitors often leave their lights on and run the air conditioning or heating even when they are gone. In other words, hotels have a large ecological footprint. Lao uses her superpowers of collaboration and problem solving to help hotels use green business practices. Lao works with her team to identify what practices can be changed and how they impact the environment. She may identify tools such as smart lighting and automatic thermostats that turn off when not in use. Once her team has the solutions, she uses her superpower of observation and communication to identify and share the ideas with hotels. She has received numerous awards, including the Sustainability Leader of the Year (2019) award.

Recharging a Whole City

ELECTRICAL ENGINEER

Where does the electricity that turns on the lights or powers the TV in your home come from? Most people never think about where their electricity comes from! In fact, most homes use electricity from a mixture of energy sources.

Electrical engineers work on the generation, transmission, and distribution of electricity. Electricity can be generated from a mixture of energy sources: burning fossil fuels, nuclear fission (splitting an atom), and renewable sources such as solar, geothermal, water, and wind energy. Power companies distribute electricity to our homes, businesses, and communities through a grid of power lines. In this complicated system, electrical engineers make sure the lights stay on! They keep the power system working efficiently. Electrical engineers are awesome at using their problem-solving skills to get power to remote locations, such as islands, or to increase the use of renewable energy.

The mixture of energy supplied to a city or town is called its **power profile**. Think about your city or town. How much energy comes from renewable or coal? What are other sources of energy? What choices do you think electrical engineers in your city or town had to make?

A........·.....·R.·......Z

Dr. Vera Silva

Dr. Vera Silva is helping to bring renewable power to the European Union (EU) grid system. In school she studied electrical engineering and spent many years doing research. Dr. Silva now leads a team of more than 3,600 engineers who work in more than seventeen countries at GE Grid Solutions. This company provides equipment and solutions to help with the electricity transmission and distribution across the globe. One of the goals of the EU is to increase the amount of electricity produced by renewable energy to 50 percent by 2030. Dr. Silva uses her superpowers of problem solving, data analysis, and communication to understand and propose ways of reaching this goal. Dr. Silva has written three books, many academic papers and often speaks at industry and academic conferences to promote the use of renewable energy sources.

Searching for Dinosaurs

PALEONTOLOGIST

What do you think dinosaur poop looks like? Is it big or small? It depends on the size of the dinosaur. Dinosaur poop fossils are called coprolites. The first female dinosaur hunter, Mary Anning, found coprolites in England. She was one of the first **paleontologists** to discover evidence of dinosaurs that led to the discovery of the Jurassic period.

Paleontologists are scientists who study **extinct** species. You may find them outside, digging up fossils, or in a lab at a university or museum. Once fossils are found, paleontologists must sometimes reassemble the pieces to identify the creature they once were. These researchers often use technology, such as magnetic resonance imaging and X-rays, to hunt for and examine fossils. Fossil data give us a clearer picture of what life on Earth looked like in the past. Paleontologists often work collaboratively to understand the species that lived here many centuries ago. Their discoveries about past life on the planet help us understand the present.

One of the best parts of discovering new fossil species is naming them. In 2018 fossil hunters named a new species after President Barack Obama. The tiny, disc-shaped creature is about half an inch long. It was one of the first species to exist on Earth but is now extinct. The creature had spiral grooves and spent most of its life underwater, where it rarely moved from its spot in the sea. Scientists named the creature Obamaus coronatus (*coronatus* means "crowned"). In fact, many presidents have fossils named after them. If you could name a fossil, who would you name it after?

Dinosaurs are not extinct. Ostriches, turkeys, and chickens are living relatives of dinosaurs. Fossils and data confirm that modern birds are direct descendants of dinosaurs. They are simply dinosaurs that adapted and evolved to fly. Next Thanksgiving, you can say, "Please pass the dinosaur," and be scientifically correct!

Dr. Lisa White

Dr. White is a geologist and a micro paleontologist. She combines her love of rocks with her profound understanding of **microorganisms** (tiny, single-celled creatures) to help understand the world of dinosaurs. Dr. White almost didn't become a scientist, but a network of incredible mentors encouraged her to pursue her work in paleomicrobiology. Now Dr. White wonders, "How many potential scientists never took earth science class simply because nobody encouraged them?" Dr. White is on a mission to change that, one student at a time, by creating what she calls "critical incidents." She uses her STEM superpowers of creativity, imagination, and communication to get young people excited about earth science by taking them on fossil hunts and geology trips. What amazing skill will you teach the next generation?

Think Global, Act Local

ENVIRONMENTAL ACTIVIST

Think about an environmental challenge facing your community. Do you have clean water? Are there many trees near you, or do you live in the dry desert? Do factories or forest fires fill the air with smoke? Communities around the world have different problems. One might struggle to get enough water for people, animals, and plants to live. Another might have a lot of fresh water but also a lot of air pollution.

There are many types of activists. Some examples are:
- political
- animal rights
- human rights
- social justice

Environmental activists are people who lead communities in solving environmental problems. Many successful environmental activists are scientists, lawyers, or engineers who have also studied science. Skills in science and math help them to understand the causes of problems and lead others in finding solutions. Have you read about plastic waste, air pollution, or endangered species? The data describing those problems might be hard to understand until an activist explains why the data matters.

Environmental activists work with whole communities to solve complicated problems. They can't do it alone! Successful activists must be able to communicate the need for change and then collaborate with others to help make that change real.

What issue would inspire you to be an activist for change? How will you use your STEM superpowers to think globally and act locally? Actively participating in your local, regional, and national community is an incredibly important part of creating a **sustainable** world.

Dr. Wangari Maathai

Kenyan biologist and veterinarian Dr. Wangari Maathai organized her community to plant tens of millions of trees throughout Kenya. Dr. Maathai observed that her communities faced environmental challenges because all the trees had been cut down for firewood. Without trees, the soil blew away, birds and animals had nowhere to live, and humans had no shade. People were struggling because they could not grow food. Combining her background in biology and her belief in helping people to help themselves, Dr. Maathai founded the Green Belt Movement. This organization aids communities by planting trees and providing jobs. Thanks to her superpowers of data analysis and collaboration, more than four million trees have been planted. Dr. Maathai became the first African woman and the only environmentalist to win a Nobel Prize. The Nobel Prize is a set of international awards given yearly to recognize scientific, academic, or cultural progress.

Uncovering the Underwater World

MARINE BIOLOGIST

Have you ever dipped your toes in the ocean? If so, you were not alone! An estimated 65 percent of all life on Earth is found in the ocean.

Marine biology is the study of organisms that live in water. This work is especially important now because human-caused climate change is affecting the health of the ocean. Marine biologists help us to understand how pollution changes the chemistry of water and affects the creatures that live in it.

Marine biologists travel around the globe, exploring the underwater world. Many spend a lot of time underwater. Whether snorkeling or scuba diving or riding in research submarines, they observe and explore our world's waters.

Amazingly, we have explored less than 10 percent of our planet's watery places. This is because much of the ocean is too deep for humans to survive. New robotic technology is helping us explore the ocean and discover all the creatures living on its floor. These robots collect samples from a variety of underwater environments that humans cannot reach. That means there are many discoveries left to be made by marine biologists. Maybe you will make some of them!

Research is an important part of STEM. Research starts with a question. Then the researcher collects observations and data and organizes, analyzes, and interprets them to help solve problems.

A·······.····.··..· U ····z

Dr. Eugenie Clark

Dr. Clark was a marine biologist who studied the underwater world and a pioneer in using scuba diving for research. While making long dives, she mastered her STEM superpower of observation to collect data from the underwater world. She also was the first person to observe how sharks sleep. She recorded that sharks don't swim when sleeping. This proved that sharks do not need to move in order to breathe. Thanks to her discoveries, Dr. Clark became known as the Shark Lady.

Viewing Germs and Viruses

MICROBIOLOGIST

Did you know there are more than one hundred *trillion* tiny bacteria living in your intestines? Or take a look in your belly button, where scientists have discovered hundreds of different species of bacteria. Don't worry: these bacteria are good for you, your body, and your health!

The scientists who study these tiny bacteria, viruses, algae, and fungi are called **microbiologists**. Microorganisms live, grow, and interact with their environments, even inside the human body. Microbiologists collect samples of these tiny critters and use microscopes to make observations and new discoveries that help create new medicines. Simply put, microbiologists save lives.

When was the last time you washed out your belly button? It is one of the dirtiest parts of the human body. Bacteria can tell us a lot about a person's health and environment. Ecological microbiologists studied sixty different belly buttons and discovered one thousand new species of bacteria. Most of the volunteers had around sixty-seven unique species in their belly button. One volunteer had a species of bacteria only found in soils in Japan.

Where Can I Find a Scientist?
Scientists aren't always stuck in laboratories like they are in the movies. The work of science happens around the globe. Pick any spot on the map, and there are scientists working there! Scientists study butterflies in the Amazon rainforest and dig up fossils in the Gobi, a desert in China. Scientists also work in governments, museums, and universities. Where do you think you might meet a scientist in your hometown?

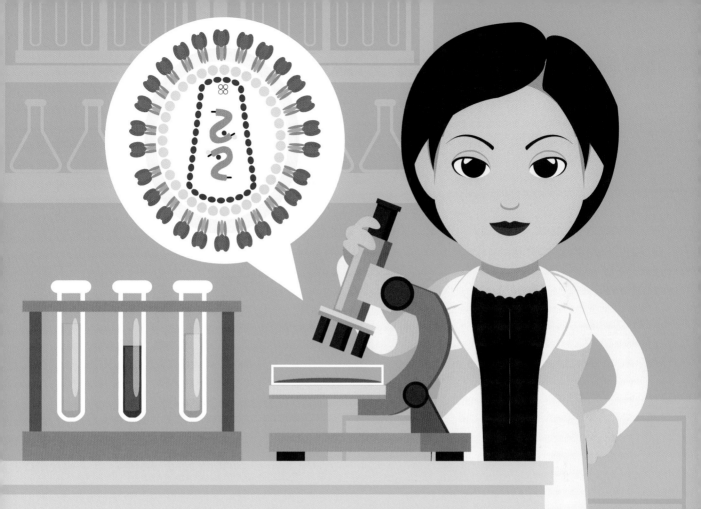

Dr. Flossie Wong-Staal

Dr. Wong-Staal is a researcher and microbiologist. She spends much of her time using her superpower of observation as she peers at viruses through her powerful microscopes. Her work has focused on one virus in particular: human immunodeficiency virus, or HIV. Her team of collaborators was the first to identify this virus as the cause of AIDS (acquired immunodeficiency syndrome). Her team helped to create the first genetic map of the HIV virus. Their data led to the development of the HIV blood tests now used to test patients for the virus. Her work saved millions of lives. Today, we consider her to be one of the top female scientists in history.

Washing Your Clothes

SUSTAINABLE FASHION DESIGNER

Where does your T-shirt come from? How did they make that shirt so colorful? The different materials used in fashion affect not only the colors and comfortableness of clothes, but also the environment. Fashion designers can use STEM to help make colorful clothing that doesn't harm the environment. Scientists study different fabrics to better understand their strengths and weaknesses. Engineers design new kinds of fabric for different uses.

A **sustainable** industry makes products without using up resources or damaging the environment. To make the fashion industry sustainable, we need superheroes with science and chemistry backgrounds. One of the environmental disasters of the twenty-first century is the use of microfibers in clothing made from types of plastic. Every time clothes are washed, tiny slivers of plastic break off. These microfibers are invisible to the human eye, but end up in our water and can now be found in the blood of fish and other aquatic creatures. When we eat these fish, microfibers end up in our blood too. Scientists have even found microfibers in the breast milk of nursing mothers! We need superheroes to create new materials for clothing that don't harm the environment or our bodies.

STEM professionals also create and use new materials for the fashion industry. Sportswear companies have designed flip flops, sneakers, and active wear using plastic from the oceans. Even jewelry lines have been designed and created from recycled waste. Many of these companies are using marketing incentives to commit to sustainable practices like removing trash from the ocean with purchases.

People throw away a lot of clothing every year. Could it be reused or **recycled?** STEM skills are part of every shirt and sock you wear. What happens to our clothes when we no longer want them? Can we recycle our clothing into something new?

A .... · · .... ω ·· z

Dr. Grace Teo

Dr. Teo is a fashion designer for people with physical disabilities. She uses her superpowers of problem solving, creativity, and collaboration at Open Style Lab, where fashion designers, engineers, and occupational therapists work together to imagine and create clothing that solves problems. First, the team talks with people who have disabilities about what they need. Occupational therapists provide more data and observations about problems that designers might not recognize. Fashion designers then envision changes, such as longer zippers, bigger buttons, or different openings that might help the wearer get dressed easily and feel comfortable. Once the idea is born, engineers and designers collaborate to create a new item of clothing. It then goes back to the people with disabilities, who test it and give the designers feedback.

Xeroxing our DNA

Have you ever eaten a seedless grape or watermelon? Did you know much of the food you eat is genetically modified? Every living organism on the planet has DNA (deoxyribonucleic acid). Segments of DNA are called **genes**. Genes carry specific information about our bodies, such as eye or hair color.

Geneticists study genes to determine how traits pass from one generation to the next. They look at the DNA of plants and animals to make new discoveries in medicine and better understand evolution on our planet. Some traits are harmless, such as baldness. Others are very dangerous, such as sickle cell anemia or a higher chance of developing cancer.

If you like biology, you might like being a geneticist. There are many different careers and branches of study in the field. Ecological geneticists study how plant and animal species adapt to their environments. Human geneticists often work in healthcare. When diseases such as HIV/AIDS, Ebola, and new flu strains are discovered, geneticists help develop medicines that save thousands and even millions of lives. Geneticists also work with police departments to help solve crimes using DNA analysis.

Every person on Earth shares 99 percent of their DNA with every other person. You also have 98 percent of your DNA in common with a chimpanzee.

Dr. Georgia M. Dunston

Dr. Dunston is a geneticist who studies the genes of Africans and people of African descent who live on other continents. Dr. Dunston founded the National Human Genome Center® at Howard University to deepen our understanding of genes specific to African Americans and other **populations** of African descent. She also analyzes genes related to health problems that affect people of African descent all over the world. Dr. Dunston's team of scientists, researchers, and geneticists collaborated to complete the Human Genome Project in 2015. This project mapped the 25,500 genes in human DNA, making it much easier to study and solve many health problems. Because of her superpowers of communication and collaboration, scientists can dig deeper into our understanding of genes to help cure hereditary diseases.

NATIONAL HUMAN GENOME CENTER

Your Computer Knows You

When you start typing something into the search window on Google or Amazon, have you noticed that it already knows what you are thinking? When watching Netflix, do you like the suggestions it provides?

These suggestions are based on a series of **algorithms**, which are mathematical instructions used to identify, analyze, and create information for users. With the right set of algorithms, a computer can use information about a user's previous searches to make informed suggestions. This learning process is part of developing **artificial intelligence (AI).** The algorithms are created by machine learning engineers.

Machine learning engineers work with computers, robots, and devices such as Siri and Alexa. AI on our devices can play music and podcasts or give us reminders to do our homework or the dishes. The future of AI is in robots and computers that can make decisions on their own. Robots might save lives by performing complicated surgeries. Self-driving cars might reduce the number of crashes. Machine learning engineers work to bring those innovations closer to reality.

What is the difference between an engineer and a scientist?
Science is about knowing. Engineering is about doing. Scientists ask questions and try to find answers. Engineers use the data produced by scientists to design and build solutions to problems. Let's look at an example of a race car. A materials scientist **investigates** and tests different materials—such as metal, rubber, and plastic—that are strong, light, flexible, and unlikely to catch fire. All these qualities are important for making cars faster and safer. An engineer then looks at the scientific data and decides what materials to use in building the actual race car.

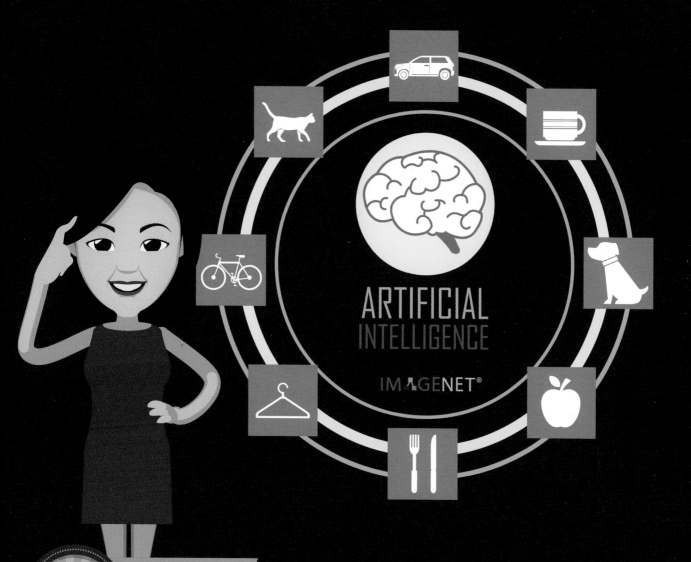

ARTIFICIAL
INTELLIGENCE

IM**A**GENET®

Dr. Fei-Fei Li

Dr. Li is leading efforts to help computers and robots see better. Robots and computers use algorithms to view and recognize images. To do this, her team uses their superpowers of collaboration and problem solving to develop algorithms that accurately describe images. These algorithms are used to accurately identify and organize the images in a virtual library. Through the virtual library ImageNet®, robots and computers can test the accuracy of the algorithms created. More than 15 million images are available on ImageNet. Today, as a professor at Stanford University, Dr. Li uses her superpower of communication to share her research and encourage emerging STEM Superheroes to pursue their interest and education in artificial intelligence and machine learning.

Zooming In on Zoology

ZOOLOGISTS

What is your favorite animal? Is it fuzzy and furry or wet and slimy? The diversity of life on Earth is amazing. Did you know that scientists estimate there are approximately 8.7 million unique species of life on Earth?

If you want to learn about all these species, you should become a **zoologist**. Zoologists study the behavior and physical characteristics of animals. They study all kinds of animals, from mammals like the zebra to the tiniest zooplankton in the sea.

Zoologists work in zoos, wildlife centers, national parks, and aquariums. They study animals in the wild. If animals are getting sick or causing problems with humans, zoologists find out why. Zoologists conduct scientific research like taking blood samples to study a virus like bird flu. They use satellites and other technology to track animal populations, including elephants, monarch butterflies, bald ibis, and cranes. Zoologists may collaborate with cartographers and use computer programs to estimate wildlife populations, understand migration and hunting patterns. Zoologist protect and preserve some of the most endangered species on our planet.

Creepy-crawly bugs, or **insects**, make up most of the life on Earth. Insects are the main food source for many animals, from hedgehogs to bats. They are a nutritious food source for many humans, too! Ants are the most numerous insects in the world: there are ten trillion or more of them. The largest insect is the giant long-horned beetle, which can be up to twenty-one centimeters long. Some insects are so small that you need a microscope to look at them: the feather-winged beetle is only 0.25 millimeters long!

The Navajo Nation Zoological and Botanical Park is the only tribally owned zoological park in the United States. It is located in Window Rock, Arizona, and labels its exhibits in the Native American Indian language of Navajo.

Which careers from this book were most interesting to you?

SUPERHERO

Cissy Kou

Imagine holding a baby panda! As a kid, Cissy Kou wanted to be a dolphin trainer or a veterinarian. Today, she is the Panda Keeper at Calgary Zoo. Kou loves that the pandas recognize her smell and her call. As a panda keeper, Kou spends her days observing and caring for the pandas. She feeds them, cleans their environment, and helps to ensure they are healthy. Kou's observations and data on the pandas will help create new generations of pandas and protect current Giant Pandas. The pandas are part of the Global Giant Panda Conservation Breeding Program.

How Do You Become an Everyday STEM Superhero?

STEM professionals make discoveries that help us understand our world. STEM professionals love to ask questions about how things work by observing the world around them. These STEM superheroes want to make the world a healthier, cleaner, and safer place by helping to find the answers to problems.

Think about some of the greatest achievements: finding water on Mars, creating the first 3D movie, designing national parks, or putting satellites into space. All of these were designed, engineered, and built by teams of everyday superheroes in STEM

You just read about twenty-six everyday superheroes in STEM. They use their superpowers to make the world a better place. You already have some of these superpowers! You can develop and practice the others.

Imagine yourself as an Everyday STEM Superhero.
Draw or write a description.

Steps to Become an Everyday STEM Superhero

☐ Daydream. Think. **Imagine**.

☐ Ask questions and think about how things work.

☐ **Observe** the world around you.

☐ Record your observations by drawing or writing.

☐ Make predictions about the world around you.

☐ Write every day: in a journal, on your cell phone, or wherever you like—just write!

☐ Read books, magazines, articles, and anything else you can get!

☐ Believe in your ability to change the world.

☐ Explore the outdoors.

☐ **Problem solve**.

☐ Design. Build. Experiment. Test. Recreate.

☐ **Collaborate** with your friends or family.

☐ **Communicate** your discoveries in writing or conversations.

☐ Make decisions based on **data**, not on how you think or feel.

Other STEM Publications by the Authors

- Sneideman, Joshua and Erin Twamley. *Climate Change: Discover How it Impacts Spaceship Earth.* Nomad Press, 2015.

- Sneideman, Joshua and Erin Twamley and others. *Energy Literacy: Essential Principles and Fundamental Concepts for Energy Education v4*, 2016.

- Sneideman, Joshua and Erin Twamley. *A guide to the energy of the Earth.* TEDEd®, 2014.

- Sneideman, Joshua and Erin Twamley. *Renewable Energy: Discover the Fuel of the Future.* Nomad Press, 2016.

- Sneideman, Joshua and Erin Twamley. *Climate Change: The Science Behind Melting Glaciers and Warming Oceans*, 2020.

- Twamley, Erin. *Capturing Cow Farts and Burps.* Waldorf Publishing, 2020.

Recommended Books

- Beaty, Andrea. *Iggy Peck, Architect* (2007); *Rosie Revere, Engineer* (2013); and *Ada Twist, Scientist* (2016), Harry N. Abrams.

- Citro, Asia. *Zoey and Sassafras* (series), The Innovation Press, 2018.

- Epsy, Stephanie. *STEM Gems: How 44 Women Shine in Science, Technology, Engineering and Mathematics, and How You Can Too!* 2016.

- Ignotofsky, Rachel. *Women in Science: 50 Fearless Pioneers Who Changed the World.* Ten Speed Press, 2016

- Keating, Jess. *Shark Lady: The True Story of How Eugenie Clark Became the Ocean's Most Fearless Scientist.* Sourcebooks Jabberwocky, 2017.

- Shipp, Brittney. *The Meteorologist in Me.* The Power of Love Books, 2016.

Everyday Superheroes Book Reviews

This book is terrific! As the mother of a daughter and a son, it's something we will read together over and over again. I'm honored to be included and hope it can help convince more young people to go into these industries by piquing their interest early in their lives.

—SUPERHERO Sonia Lo, Vertical Farmer

A much-awaited resource for parents and educators designed to guide learning and explore the world of the STEM fields. The Everyday Superheroes within these pages are real-world, accomplished professionals that all children can relate to and envision themselves as in their future. A must-have book for every home and library!

—Nancy J. Watson, M.Ed.,
Director of STEM Professional Development and Programs

This resource is a wonderful addition to any educator or parent library for cultivating a rich STEM career environment. Learners of all ages will begin to discover a variety of paths to be involved in STEM leadership post-high school. The focus on women is especially needed today to encourage young women to pursue their passions for shaping our world.

—Claire McGee, District Lead STEAM Coach,
Metro Nashville Public Schools

Whether you look to the skies with dreams of space exploration or peer into a microscope to get a closer look at the life that blooms in the tiny crevices of our world, this book will inspire you with a variety of paths to explore with Science, Technology, Engineering, and Mathematics! Explore the world, look with eyes filled with curiosity and wonder, and discover a world of Women in STEM who bring these dreams of science and technology to life!

—Amy Oyler, The Scientific Mom

Everyday Superheroes Book Reviews Cont'd

This is a timeless work of art that is desperately needed for a 21st century learner. I believe that works like this will bring people back to a place where the imagination can guide opportunity rather than a reliance on existing innovation. From one's imagination, comes innovation—just look inside.

—Dr. Pamela Hampton-Garland Ph.D.,
University of the District of Columbia

Twamley and Sneideman have created another great book for kids with *Everyday Superheroes: Women in STEM Careers*. With easy-to-read and understandable text and vibrant engaging illustrations, they bring yesterday's and today's STEM Superheroes to life alongside a very comprehensive list of many of today's STEM careers! It's almost a shame that the alphabet only had 26 letters limiting them to 26 careers. This book will inspire, educate, and engage today's kids (and some parents too) to learn more about the world around them and the careers ahead of them. It belongs in every classroom, on every nightstand, and in every backpack.

—Mary Spruill, Executive Director, The NEED Project
(National Energy Education Development Project)

For parents of young daughters interested in science and seeking to find cool women to read about, this book solves both curiosities in a really engaging way. Adults will love reading this book with their kids and learn a lot too! Kids will like the connection and stories of real women engaged in these careers.

—Linda Silverman, Former Solar Decathlon Director,
Department of Energy

The attention to describing the careers as well as giving real life examples is absolutely incredible. This book provides concrete examples for students and anyone wanting to know more about STEM careers and their impact on the world.

—Rebecca Norton, Special Education Science Teacher

Everyday Superheroes Book Reviews Cont'd

The authors have created an inspirational and accessible resource that will be particularly valuable for girls at a critical time in their educational life. It is an important contribution that will help ignite both boys' and girls' imaginations, especially for students who wander into a valley of disinterest that may divert them from pursuing STEM. It helps connect the dots from school subjects to real-world professions and answers the perennial *Why should I care?* question. I highly recommend this book to students, parents, teachers, librarians, and career counselors alike.

—Dr. Michelle Fox, Educator and Technologist

Wow! While this book is designed for elementary and middle school kids, I learned a lot about STEM careers myself as well. The short bios about diverse women in STEM explained the latest technology in a clear, interesting manner. The artwork and graphics are very attractive and complement the writing.

—Dr. Charles Robinson, Charles Robinson, Ed.D.,
International Education, Framingham (MA) State University

From Earth's crust to outer space, and to all corners of the world, this book covers a vast array of STEM themes. The themes are presented in logical and captivating ways, making the book interesting and easy to understand. There is also a plethora of rich STEM vocabulary words to be learned. The interactive pull-outs add practical experience to theories and concepts. Very educational for a wide range of ages and levels.

—Denis Sauve, Educator, B.S. / B.Ed. / M.Ed. / M.Ed.

If you're hoping to spark curiosity in STEM career paths among youth, check out *Everyday Superheroes*. The creative approach to everyday problem-solving as a "STEM superhero" is a great way to start conversations with young audiences. The range of roles covered offers a variety of entry points: from Director of Sustainability to Sustainable Fashion Designer, the book shows that wherever your interest may be, you can always use STEM problem-solving to be a force for better in our world.

—Christina Leavell, Midwest Regional Hub Leader,
National Informal STEM Education Network (NISE Net)

Glossary

#

3D animation: the process of using movement to make drawings, models, or inanimate objects come to life

A

accurate: correct in all details; exact

activist: a person who argues for change

aerospace engineer: a person who designs and builds aircraft and spacecraft

algorithm: a set of instructions used by a robot or computer

analysis: close and careful study

artificial intelligence (AI): an area of computer science that creates human-like machines

astronomer: a person who studies objects outside Earth's atmosphere, such as the sun, moon, planets, and stars

atmosphere: the mixture of gases surrounding a planet

B

biomedical engineer: a person who solves problems related to biology or medicine by designing processes and devices

biometric: data related to body measurements and calculations

C

career: a job that someone does for a long time

cartographer: a person who creates maps

civil engineer: a person who designs, constructs, or maintains human-built environments, including roads, bridges, canals, dams, airports, sewage systems, pipelines, and railways

climate: the usual weather conditions of a region—such as temperature, air pressure, humidity, precipitation, sunshine, cloudiness, and winds—throughout the year, averaged over a series of years

collaboration: to work with others

communication: the exchange of information by speaking, listening, or writing community: a group of people who live in the same area

conservation: the careful or reduced use of something

consumption: use of a resource

cosmos: everything that exists in our universe, including galaxies

curiosity: strong desire to know or learn something

Curiosity: a car-sized rover exploring Mars for NASA

D

data: points of information you observe or collect, often in the form of numbers

design: to plan and sketch out something before it is made

E

ecological footprint: the impact of a person or community on the environment

efficiency: use without waste

energy: the ability to do work

engineer: a person who uses their skills and imagination to build things

engineering: a branch of STEM that focuses on the design, building, and use of engines, machines, and structures

environment: everything in nature, living and nonliving, including plants, animals, soil, rocks, water, and air

extinct: no longer in existence, having no living members

F

financial analyst: a person who collects and analyzes data about the money of companies and helps to develop a plan about costs and investments

fossil: the remains or traces of ancient plants or animals left in rock

fossil fuels: coal, oil, and natural gas. These energy sources come from the fossils of plants and microorganisms that lived millions of years ago

G

gene: a part of your DNA that is transferred from a parent to child and determines some of the child's characteristics like eye and hair color

geneticist: a scientist who studies how traits are passed at the molecular, organism, or population level geologist: a scientist who studies the history, structure, and origin of the earth

Global Positioning System (GPS): a radio navigation system that allows people on land, at sea, or in the air to determine their exact location

H

habitat: the natural home or environment of an animal, plant, or other organism

I

imagination: the ability to form new ideas or images; the ability of the mind to be creative or resourceful

impact: an effect or influence

indigenous: natural in a particular place; native

insect: a kind of animal that has three body parts and six legs

invent: to create something new

investigate: to gather data about an object or event

M

math: the study of quantity, structure, physical space, and change

mathematician: a person who solves problems using math

mean: the average of a set of numbers

median: the middle number in a set of numbers

meteorologist: a person who studies the atmosphere, weather, and climate

microbiologist: a person who studies the growth, structure, and development of microscopic organisms, such as bacteria, algae, or fungi

microorganism: a living creature that requires a microscope or magnifying glass to see, especially a bacterium, virus, or fungus

mineral: a natural solid found in rocks and in the ground

mode: the number which appears most often in a set of numbers

N

natural resources: things found in nature that are useful to humans, such as water to drink, trees to burn, and fish to eat

O

observation: to use your five senses to experience something

orbit: to circle another object in space

organism: a living thing

oxygen: a gas found in the air that people and animals need to breathe to stay alive

P

paleontologist: a scientist who studies fossils

park ranger: a person who plans, develops, and conducts programs to inform people about the science, history, and natural features of national, state, or local parks

photosynthesis: the process by which green plants use sunlight to synthesize foods from carbon dioxide and water

pollution: substances in the environment that can harm living things or damage natural resources

population: all the living things of one kind in an area or in a group

power profile: an outline of how and where your electricity is generated

precipitation: water that falls to Earth's surface as rain, snow, sleet, or hail

predict: to state what you think will happen based on observations or data

problem solving: finding solutions using creativity, design, and testing

professional: a person engaged in a specific job field

R

record: to write something down in order to communicate findings with other people

recycle: to reuse something by shredding, squashing, pulping, or melting to use the materials to create new products

renewable energy: a form of energy that doesn't get used up including energy from the sun or wind

research: the process of studying data and information to establish facts and reach conclusions

robotics: the branch of technology that deals with the design, construction, operation of robots

S

satellite: a human made object placed in orbit around the earth, the moon, or another planet in order to collect data or help with communication

science: the study of the natural world

skill: a type of work or activity that requires special training or knowledge

soil: tiny pieces of rock, minerals, and decayed plant and animal matter solar system: the collection of planets and their moons in orbit around a sun, together with smaller bodies in the form of asteroids, meteoroids, comets, and dwarf planets. Our solar system's planets are Mercury, Venus, Earth, Mars, Jupiter, Saturn, Uranus, and Neptune

solution: an answer to a problem

source: the place from which food or energy comes

species: a group of living organisms consisting of similar individuals capable of exchanging reproduction

STEM: acronym used for the fields of study in science, technology, engineering, and mathematics

sustainable: a process or material that is not harmful to the environment

system: a set of connected parts working together

T

technology: a field of STEM that uses scientific knowledge

telescope: a scientific instrument used to look at distant objects

temperature: how hot or cold something is

V

vertical farm: a space for food to grow on vertical surfaces, such as shelves or buildings

Z

zoologist: a scientist who studies animals and their habitats

zooplankton: small and microscopic animals drifting or floating in the sea or freshwater

About the Authors

Erin Twamley and Joshua Sneideman are educators and authors of STEM publications from blogs to children's books (*Climate Change: Discover How It Impacts Spaceship Earth* and *Renewable Energy: Discover the Fuel of the Future*).

Erin Twamley is passionate about providing STEM learning opportunities. Through her STEM publications, she aims to highlight the leadership and discoveries of women and diverse communities. Twamley leads STEM and Author Encounters with Department of Defense Education Activity, international schools, and Girl Scouts. She loves to travel and read and has lived on three continents.

Joshua Sneideman is an innovative educator who provides professional development for schools and teachers around the country on best practices in STEM. As the Albert Einstein Distinguished Educator Fellow at the Department of Energy, he led national STEM and energy literacy efforts. His STEM publications include three STEM education children's books, two TED-Ed cartoons, and multiple articles on STEM education. Sneideman taught middle school math and science for ten years around the world. When not in the office, you are most likely to find him teaching young people to race sailboats or working on his next book!

Together, the authors engage the next generation of learners in protecting and creating a sustainable planet through STEM literacy. Reach the authors to schedule a virtual or in-person author encounter. Connect on social media to share your STEM Superhero!

About the Illustrator Collective

A collaboration of powerful artists from around the world contributed to make these awesome superhero profiles. These women and men are dedicated to sharing their artistry and have a commitment to sharing in diversity. Thank you to Buyung Nugroho for making the STEM superheroes come to life. We appreciate their detail and commitment to bringing these STEM superheroes' colorful stories and images to life.

Share your STEM Superhero!

f @STEMSuperhero • **P** @ErinEDU • **🐦** @STEMsuperheros

🌐 erinedu.org • ✉ stemsuperhero365@gmail.com